Common Core Lessons & Activities:
The United States Constitution

By Carole Marsh

Published by Gallopade International, Inc.

Printed in the U.S.A. (Peachtree City, Georgia)

TABLE OF CONTENTS

G: Includes Graphic Organizer
GO: Graphic Organizer is also available 8½" x
download at www.gallopade.com/client/go
(numbers above correspond to the graphic organizer numbers online)

Articles of Confederation

Read the text and answer the questions.

The Articles of Confederation are known as the first U.S. Constitution. They were a list of rules meant to govern and unify the states. The Articles were ratified by all 13 states in March 1781, five years after the Continental Congress first began writing them.

The Articles were written on the heels of America winning the Revolutionary War against Great Britain. Therefore, it is no surprise that the Articles reflected a fear of big government. The Articles provided for a weak central government and gave considerable power to the states.

The Articles of Confederation gave Congress power to make laws but not the power to enforce them. The legislature had to get approval from nine states to pass any laws—a difficult task because the states did not often agree.

James Madison believed the Articles were not strong enough. Only a strong central government, he felt, could support the nation and defend it. Spain and Great Britain were still a threat, the economy was suffering, and states were turning against each other.

Madison believed that states should be given power—just not to the detriment of the nation as a whole. He wrote: "Let it be tried whether any middle ground can be taken which will at once support a due supremacy of the national authority."

From May to September 1787, delegates to the Constitutional Convention in Philadelphia met to revise the Articles. George Mason, a delegate from Virginia, wrote: "The eyes of the United States are turned upon this Assembly and their Expectations raised to a very anxious Degree."

PART A: Use the text to infer whether each statement is **true** or **false**. Write **T** for true and **F** for false. Correct all false statements.

1. ______ Work on writing the Articles of Confederation began in 1781.
2. ______ The Articles of Confederation were the first U.S. Constitution.
3. ______ Congress could only pass laws if all states agreed.
4. ______ The purpose of the convention was to revise the Articles.

PART B: Use a dictionary or context to define each word or phrase as it is used in the text.

5. <u>on the heels of</u>
6. <u>threat</u>
7. <u>detriment</u>
8. <u>middle ground</u>

PART C: Read the quotations. Then explain what each quote means in your own words.

9. "Let it be tried whether any middle ground can be taken which will at once support a due supremacy of the national authority."
10. "The eyes of the United States are turned upon this Assembly and their Expectations raised to a very anxious Degree."

PART D: Determine whether each statement is **fact** or **opinion**. Write **F** for fact and **O** for opinion.

11. ______ The United States adopted its first written constitution in 1781.
12. ______ A big central government is a threat to the rights of all states.
13. ______ The Continental Congress could make laws, but the Articles did not give Congress the power to enforce them.
14. ______ The nation could not be defended from foreign attack without a strong central government.
15. ______ Spain and Great Britain were still a threat.

BONUS: Answer the following questions.

16. Explain why the authors of the Articles of Confederation favored a weak central government and gave power to the states. Cite evidence from the text to support your answer.
17. What were the obstacles Congress faced under the Articles of Confederation? Explain how these obstacles made it difficult for the Congress to run the country.

COMPARE & CONTRAST

Constitutional Correspondence

These texts are paraphrased excerpts from longer letters between John Jay and George Washington in 1786 on the topic of revising the Articles of Confederation.

Read the texts and answer the questions.

> Our national government has some very real problems that threaten "to blast the fruit we expected from our 'Tree of Liberty'." More and more of our leaders in government have the opinion that a General Convention is needed to revise the Articles of Confederation. Whether the people are ready for this or not is anyone's guess.
>
> John Jay to George Washington—March 16, 1786

> I absolutely agree with you, Sir, that the government is facing some real challenges. I would be surprised if a solution existed at this time. This situation is serious, but I fear that the people are not ready to make changes. I doubt that a Convention would make a difference. There is no doubt in my mind, however, that the Articles need revising. Something must be done—and fast!
>
> George Washington to John Jay—May 18, 1786

1. What is the meaning of John Jay's expression "to blast the fruit we expected from our 'tree of liberty' "? Is it positive or negative?
2. What is the common theme shared by both letters? Cite specific statements from the text to support your answer.
3. On what fact do both John Jay and George Washington agree? Cite specific statements from the texts to support your answer.
4. Compare and contrast the attitudes of the authors on holding a general convention. Cite specific phrases that support your conclusions.
5. Based on the text, how do you think John Jay would respond to George Washington's letter? Discuss in small groups and work together to draft John Jay's response. Share your response with the class.

Virginia Plan v. Hamilton's Plan

From May to September 1787, delegates from 12 of the 13 states met in Philadelphia to discuss how to revise the Articles of Confederation. Two of the plans that were proposed regarding state representation are paraphrased and summarized below.

Read the texts and answer the questions.

The Virginia Plan

The Articles are sorely inadequate to govern this great nation of ours. What this country needs is a strong central government. What I propose is a government comprised of three branches—the legislative, executive, and judicial. What's more, this new government would have veto power over laws that are passed in the states. This plan means "a strong consolidated union in which the idea of states should be nearly annihilated."

—Virginia Governor Edmund Randolph, May 29, 1787

Hamilton's Plan (The British Plan)

I would like to say that the British government is "the best in the world." I propose that "an executive" should lead our great country for life, with good behavior. This person would have full veto power over all laws, and senate members would have the power to pass "all laws whatsoever." They would serve for life, with good behavior. My proposal is by far the best plan for our new nation!

—Alexander Hamilton, June 18, 1787

1. A. Define consolidated as it is used in the text.
   B. What does Randolph mean by a "strong consolidated union"?
2. Compare and contrast the two plans. What was the purpose of each?
3. In your opinion, which is the stronger plan? In a well-organized essay, defend your point of view. Include any changes you would make to the plan and explain. Proofread and edit your response before sharing with the class.

The Great Compromise

Read the text and answer the questions.

The delegates to the 1787 Constitutional Convention had to decide how individual states would be represented in Congress.

The Virginia Plan proposed a bicameral legislature, which included two houses of Congress. The number of representatives in each house would be based on proportional representation. This meant that a state's population determined how many representatives it would have in Congress. Delegates from populated states would be well represented, while small states like Delaware believed they would be underrepresented in Congress. To small states, this plan was a direct threat to their states' rights. They believed they would be out voted on issues that were important to them. They wanted more from this new Constitution!

William Paterson of New Jersey proposed the New Jersey Plan that included a unicameral legislature. This plan gave each state equal representation. The plan would leave most of the Articles of Confederation in place, but it would give Congress more power.

The New Jersey Plan was rejected in favor of the Virginia Plan, but delegates from the small states threatened to leave the Convention. Debate continued until July 16, when a compromise was finally reached.

The Great Compromise, proposed by Roger Sherman of Connecticut, blended the Virginia and New Jersey Plans. It was the perfect solution to many. The compromise stated that Congress would be made up of a Senate and a House of Representatives. Each state would have an equal number of Senators, but the number of representatives in the House of Representatives would be based on a state's population.

Both large and small states agreed to the Great Compromise and the first article of the Constitution was written to divide the legislative branch into the Senate and the House of Representatives. This solution is still in use today.

PART A: Use the text to infer whether each statement is true of the Virginia Plan or the New Jersey Plan. Write **V** for Virginia Plan and **N** for New Jersey Plan.

1. ______ The plan proposed a unicameral legislature.
2. ______ Both Houses of the legislature would be based on population.
3. ______ The plan was popular with small states.

PART B: Answer the questions related to the text's vocabulary.

4. What is meant by states' rights? Whose state's rights were most threatened by the Virginia Plan?
5. Define proposed by giving a synonym.
6. Which words and phrases in the text help define the meaning of proportional representation? Why did small states oppose it?
7. Summarize the key difference between unicameral and bicameral.
8. Use a dictionary to define compromise. What part of speech is it as used in the text?

PART C: Read each statement and determine whether a **small** state or a **large** state was **most likely** to have said it. Write **S** for small state and **L** for large state. Use the text to help determine your answer.

9. ______ "A bicameral legislature with representation based on population in both houses of Congress is the best for all states!"
10. ______ "This plan is a direct threat to states' rights. We will be underrepresented in Congress!"
11. ______ "They say they will be outvoted in Congress, but what they are really looking for is power!"
12. ______ "At least one of the houses should have equal representation for every state!"

PART D: Read the statement made by Benjamin Franklin during the Constitutional Convention on the issue of state representation. What concept is he suggesting? Cite evidence from the text to explain how his statement applies to the state representation solution.

"When a broad table is to be made, and the planks do not fit, the artist takes a little from both, and makes a good joint."

Federalists v. Antifederalists

Read the text, complete the graphic organizer, and answer the questions.

In the late 1700s, the young country was divided over the issue of a new Constitution. Most politicians were Federalists. They recognized that the Articles of Confederation were weak. They wanted a constitution with a stronger central government that could regulate the activities of the states. Generally, Federalists were wealthier aristocrats. On the other hand, some politicians were Antifederalists. Antifederalists were typically of a lower class. They feared state regulation and worried that a central government could easily abuse its powers. The Antifederalists' strongest argument against ratifying the Constitution was a lack of a bill of rights.

The final draft of the Constitution, sent to the states for approval, favored a strong central government. Federalists thought a central government could more easily compete in the world market, protect the nation from foreign threat, and unify the states. However, Federalists compromised with Antifederalists to limit the government's power. Thus, the Constitution includes a separation of powers, a system of checks and balances, and a bill of rights.

Federalists:		**Antifederalists:**
	V.	

1. Why did the Antifederalists fear a strong central government? Do you agree with their point of view? Why or why not?
2. According to the text, what benefits come from having a strong central government? Predict what problems might arise without a strong central government.
3. Antifederalists were the first promoters of "states' rights." Is this issue still relevant today? Use an online resource to research examples.

PRIMARY SOURCE ANALYSIS

Article I

These excerpts from the first article of the Constitution describe the basic organization and qualifications of the Legislative Branch.

Read the text and answer the questions.

Article I excerpts

1) "All legislative Powers herein granted shall be vested in a Congress of the United States, which shall consist of a Senate and House of Representatives."
2) "The House of Representatives shall be composed of Members chosen every second Year by the People of the several states.... Representatives and direct Taxes shall be apportioned among the several States... according to their respective [population]..."
3) "No Person shall be a Representative who shall not have attained to the Age of twenty five Years, and been seven Years a Citizen of the United States..."
4) "The Senate of the United States shall be composed of two Senators from each State, chosen by the Legislature thereof for six Years and each Senator shall have one Vote."
5) "No Person shall be a Senator who shall not have attained to the Age of thirty Years, and been nine Years a Citizen of the United States..."

1. What is the purpose of Section 1? Infer the meaning of "legislative Powers."
2. A. What is the minimum age requirement to be elected to the House of Representatives? What is the minimum age for a Senator?
   B. How often are Senators elected into office? How often are House Representatives elected into office?
3. Explain how Roger Sherman's Great Compromise directly influenced Article I of the Constitution.
4. In your opinion, why must a member of Congress first be a U.S. citizen?

Purpose of the Constitution

Read the text and answer the questions.

In 1789, the Constitution was ratified without any amendments. Initially, the Constitution created the office of the President, established the Supreme Court, and allowed Congress to create laws, levy taxes on the people, and defend the country. The Constitution also gave all citizens equal rights in every state and allowed trade throughout the country. Overall, the Constitution created a stronger central government than allowed by the Articles of Confederation.

The Constitution was also written to give power to the people. The Preamble to the United States Constitution begins with three words: "We the People." These words may seem insignificant, but they are very meaningful! They indicate that the government's power comes from people who vote and contribute to the political government. The idea that people rule the government, and not the other way around, is called popular sovereignty.

When the Constitution was written, the colonies had only recently won their independence from Great Britain to become independent states. They did not want to create a government that would take away their rights like King George III had done. By giving power to the people, the Constitution helped create a limited government. The Constitution protects the rights of the people and limits the power of the government to control the people.

These limitations on government were important to many Constitutional delegates who were afraid of a powerful central government. Some states only ratified the Constitution on the condition a bill of rights would be added later to protect individual and state freedoms. In December of 1791, the first ten amendments to the Constitution (The Bill of Rights) were ratified by all 13 states and became law. Today, the U.S. Constitution is made up of 7 articles and 27 amendments.

PART A: Use the text to infer whether each statement is **true** or **false**. Write **T** for true and **F** for false.

1. ______ The Constitution was ratified without a bill of rights.
2. ______ The Constitution gave the Supreme Court the power to create laws and taxes.
3. ______ The Preamble to the Constitution gives the government unlimited powers over the people.
4. ______ The Bill of Rights was ratified to protect the freedoms of states and individuals from the central government.

PART B: Use information from the text to answer the questions.

5. What is the main idea of the first paragraph?
6. List the parts of government created by the Constitution.
7. What powers were given to Congress by the Constitution?
8. Use the text to explain the concept of popular sovereignty.
9. Explain the relationship between popular sovereignty and limited government. Cite evidence from the text to support your answer.
10. How did the recent events of the American Revolution influence the purpose of writing the Constitution?
11. Why might it be important that all citizens in every state have equal rights?

PART C: Complete the writing and speaking activities.

12. Write an essay on the topic, "We the People." In your own words, explain the importance of popular sovereignty in the United States. Proofread and edit your work.
13. Imagine that you are part of a committee presenting the U.S. Constitution to the people of America for the first time. In your own words, write a short speech explaining the purpose of the Constitution and the powers that it gives. Present your speech and answer any questions about the new Constitution.

From Articles to Amendments

The graphic organizer features steps that contributed to the ratification of the United States Constitution and the Bill of Rights that followed. Beside each step, write its significance. The first answer is provided for you.

Step	Significance
Three-Fifths Compromise	
Checks and Balances	
Separation of Powers	
The Great Compromise	
Constitutional Convention	
Articles of Confederation	Articles created a weak central government and a loose friendship of states.

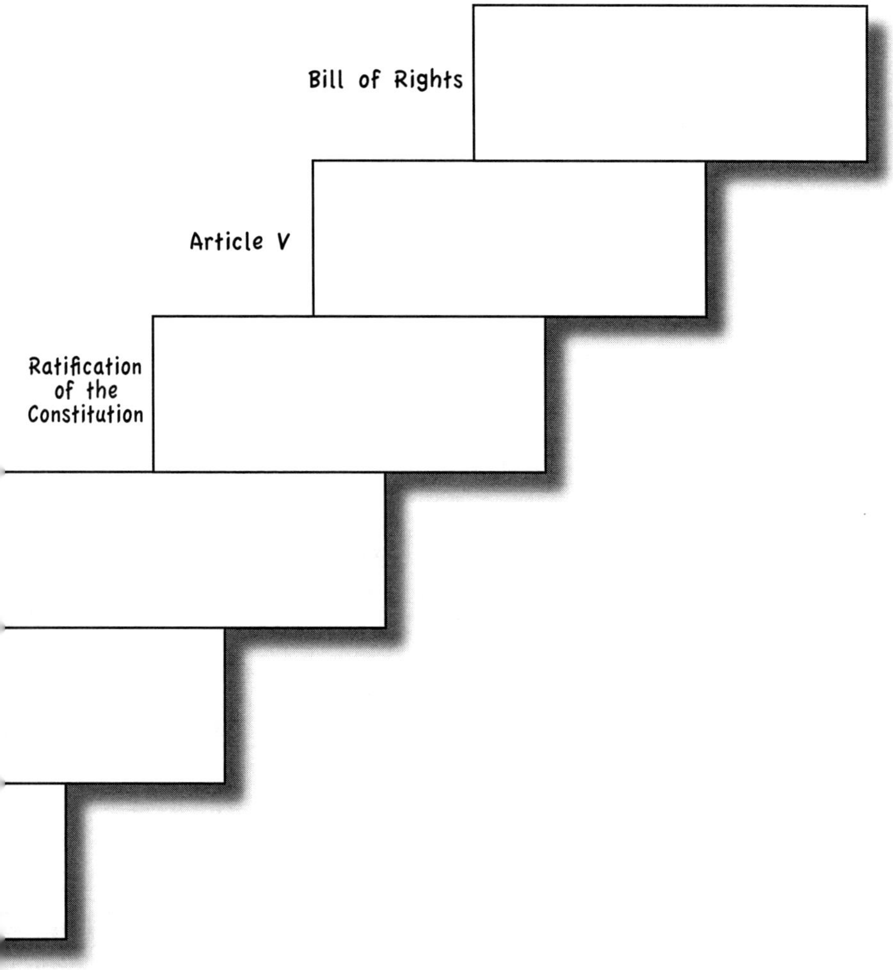
Bill of Rights
Article V
Ratification of the Constitution

Constitutional Vocabulary

Use a dictionary or online resource to define the terms and explain how each is significant to the U.S. Constitution.

Vocabulary	Definition	Significance to the U.S. Constitiution
central government		
checks and balances		
compromise		
federalism		
limited government		
popular sovereignty		
Preamble		
separation of powers		
states' rights		

PROBLEM-SOLUTION-RESULTS

The Preamble

The Preamble to the Constitution was carefully worded by the delegates to the 1787 Constitutional Convention. The Preamble reveals the determination of the framers of the Constitution to avoid the same problems the states encountered under the Articles of Confederation.

Read the Preamble to the U.S. Constitution. Write each underlined phrase in the Preamble next to the problem it addresses.

Preamble

We the People of the United States, in Order to form a more perfect Union, establish Justice, insure domestic Tranquility, provide for the common defense, promote the general Welfare, and secure the Blessings of Liberty to ourselves and our Posterity, do ordain and establish this Constitution for the United States of America.

1. ________________________ Under the Articles of Confederation, the central government had no power to defend U.S. citizens from attack or to protect its borders.

2. ________________________ Under the Articles of Confederation, the central government could not prevent problems between states, such as states placing tariffs on goods "exported" to other states.

3. ________________________ Under the Articles of Confederation, the central government could do little to protect the freedom the country had fought so hard for. Freedom for future generations was at stake.

4. ________________________ Article IV of the Articles of Confederation provided for an ineffective system of settling disputes between states because there was no national court system to interpret the laws.

5. ________________________ Under the Articles of Confederation, the central government had no enforceable system of taxation to raise money to provide services to its citizens.

READING INFORMATIONAL TEXT

Separation of Powers

Read the text and answer the questions.

The delegates at the Constitutional Convention in Philadelphia designed the new Constitution so that no branch of government would have too much power.

James Madison said, "The accumulation of all powers, legislative, executive, and judiciary, in the same hands, whether of one, a few, or many, and whether hereditary, self-appointed, or elective, may justly be pronounced the very definition of tyranny."

Articles I through III of the Constitution outline the powers and responsibilities of the three distinct branches of the U.S. government. The first article deals with the legislative branch, the second, the executive branch, and the third, the judicial branch.

The legislative branch consists of Congress, which is made up of the House of Representatives and the Senate. This branch is responsible for making the laws, levying taxes, and providing defense for the nation.

The executive branch is headed by the president and is responsible for enforcing the laws. The president has the executive veto power and is considered the Commander in Chief.

The judicial branch includes the Supreme Court and is responsible for interpreting the laws. The Supreme Court often sets important guidelines for how the laws are followed.

1. Use a dictionary to define tyranny. Summarize James Madison's quotation in your own words.
2. According to the text, what was the purpose of separating powers among different branches of government?
3. What historical events influenced the states to avoid the creation of a strong central government with no separation of powers?
4. In your opinion, does the separation of power help or hinder the government from making decisions? As a class, share your points of view.

Checks and Balances

Separation of powers guarantees that no one branch of government has all the power. Each branch has different responsibilities and has the power to "check" or "balance" the power of another branch. The diagram illustrates these checks and balances.

Look at the diagram and label the executive, legislative, and judicial branches of the U.S. government. Then answer the questions.

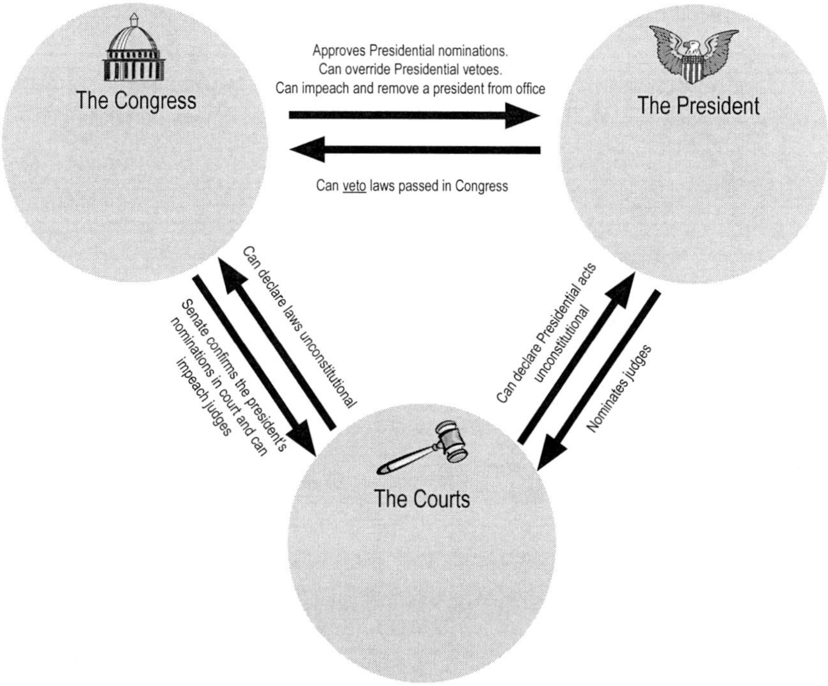

1. A. Use a dictionary to define veto.
   B. What powers does the president have over the Judicial Branch?
2. What is the common purpose of separation of powers and checks and balances? How are they different?
3. Using the diagram to support your answer, give three examples of why checks and balances were included in the Constitution.
4. Outline a realistic series of steps illustrating the systems of separation of power and checks and balances beginning, "The President nominates John Smith for Supreme Court Justice."

Father of the Constitution

James Madison became recognized as the Father of the Constitution later on in life because of his tireless work on the United States Constitution.

In your own words, explain the effect of James Madison's contributions to the Constitution. The first answer is provided for you.

Contribution		Effect
"I helped write the Virginia Constitution in 1776. It was well thought out and detailed."	→	The 1776 Virginia Constitution, or Virginia Plan, was used as a basic framework for the U.S. Constitution.
"Once we sent the final draft of the Constitution to the states for approval, or ratification, I co-wrote the Federalist Papers, which were essays to convince the states that a strong central government was necessary and to go ahead and approve the Constitution."	→	
"At the First Congress, I urged my fellow Congressmen to remember the promise we made to the states to add a Bill of Rights to the Constitution."	→	
"Twelve of the seventeen amendment proposals I made passed in both houses of Congress and then went on to the states for ratification."	→	

Slavery and Compromise

Read the text and answer the questions.

During the 1787 Constitutional Convention, two major slavery debates were resolved through compromise.

The first compromise dealt with representation in Congress. Southern delegates to the Convention feared that the first draft of the Constitution did not give their states equal representation in Congress. Southern states had fewer citizens than northern states. Delegates from the South proposed allowing slaves to count toward their population. Northern delegates argued that slaves were property and shouldn't be counted toward a state's population.

The Three-Fifths Compromise allowed southern states to count three-fifths of their slaves toward their state's total population. A larger population meant more voting power in Congress.

The second compromise had to do with the slave trade and commerce. Primarily, Northern delegates wanted the slave trade to end, while many Southern delegates argued that slavery was vital to the region's economy. In addition, Southern delegates did not want Congress to impose tariffs on imported and exported goods because their economy was heavily reliant on trade. Northerners promoted tariffs because if imported goods were more expensive, people would buy U.S. products.

The Commerce and Slave Trade Compromise allowed Congress to tax imports (including slaves) but not exports. It also supported the slave trade for 20 years, after which Congress could ban it.

1. Explain why the Three-Fifths Compromise was important to the South. Predict the outcome had no compromise been made in Congress.
2. In your opinion, were these compromises fair? Why or why not?
3. Minister Samuel Hopkins wrote:

   "These States, who have been fighting for liberty... cannot agree in any political Constitution, unless it indulge and authorize them to enslave their fellow men..."

   Rewrite the quote in your own words. Cite evidence from both compromises that supports Mr. Hopkins' observation. What do you think his opinion on slavery was, and why?

MAP ACTIVITY

Ratification of the U.S. Constitution

Use the map and data to answer the questions.

Ratification of the United States Constitution Results:

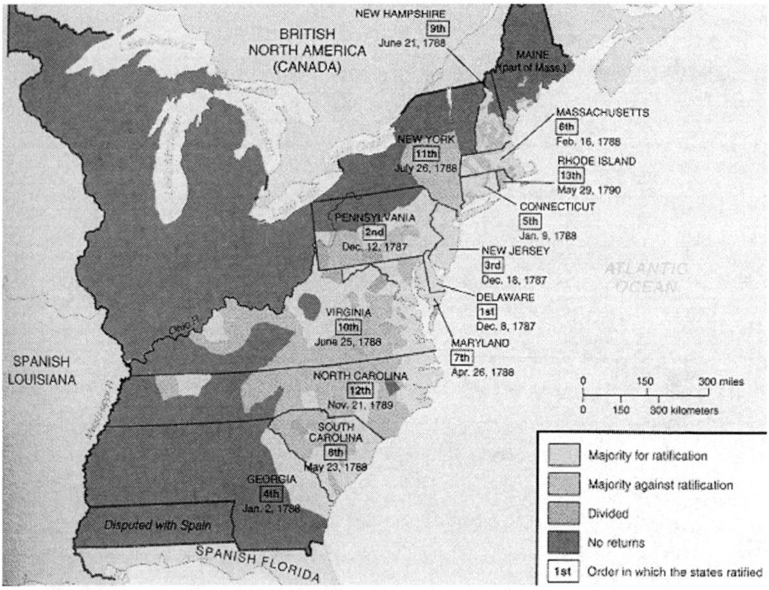

1. What do you notice about the boundaries of the thirteen states?
2. Which state was the first to ratify the new Constitution? Which state was last to ratify? What can you infer about these states?
3. At least a full two-thirds of the 13 states had to ratify the Constitution before it could go into effect. How many states were needed to ratify the Constitution, according to this rule?
4. Delaware is a small state. Predict how Delaware would have voted had the Great Compromise not been agreed upon by the delegates of the Constitutional Convention.
5. What does this map indicate about westward expansion at the time of the ratification of the Constitution?

Bill of Rights Quotes

The final draft of the Constitution passed in Congress without a Bill of Rights. During the first Congress, James Madison urged his fellow congressmen to consider adding a bill of rights. These quotations are opinions about considering a bill of rights.

Rewrite each quote in your own words to complete the graphic organizer and answer the questions.

Quotes:	What each quote means to me:
"[A] bill of rights is what the people are entitled to against every government on earth, general or particular, and what no just government should refuse, or rest on inference." --Thomas Jefferson, Dec 1787	
"We owe it to these people. We didn't make it conditional. But we did make an honorable promise. We did agree to consider this issue in order to quell the fears of those who would otherwise support the Constitution. It is an important part of the democratic process to seek unity if possible. So I'm bringing it to you." --James Madison, 1789	

1. Identify the common theme between the two quotes. What words/ phrases support your conclusion?
2. Summarize Jefferson and Madison's arguments for considering a bill of rights. How are they different?
3. In your opinion, which quote is more persuasive? Explain.
4. Natural rights are those rights to life, liberty, and the pursuit of happiness. Explain the relationship between Jefferson's quotation and natural rights.
5. Agree or disagree with the statement, "it is an important part of the democratic process to seek unity," and support your point of view.

Amending the Constitution

Read the text and answer the questions.

Amending the Constitution is an important process described in the U.S. Constitution. Article V of the Constitution lists two ways to amend the U.S. Constitution. The most popular method involves approval by the United States Congress and by the states.

Both houses of Congress (the Senate and the House of Representatives) must pass a proposal for an Amendment by a two-thirds majority. The proposal then goes on to the states for ratification.

Three-fourths of the state legislatures must pass the proposal before it can become an amendment. To pass a proposal in a state legislature requires only a simple majority of votes.

Historically, proposing and ratifying an amendment is a difficult process. Since 1789, over 11,000 proposals have been made to amend the Constitution. Only 27 proposals have been ratified by three-fourths of the state legislatures as amendments to the Constitution. The first ten amendments (Bill of Rights) were all proposed and ratified between 1789 and 1791.

1. Answer the following questions about vocabulary in the text.
   A. What is a synonym for proposal?
   B. Explain the meaning of ratification.
   C. Explain the difference between a two-thirds majority and a simple majority.
2. According to the text, what parts of the government are involved in ratifying amendments to the Constitution? Explain the process.
3. What is another name for first ten amendments?
4. Why do you think the delegates of the Constitutional Convention thought it important to make the amendment process difficult? Explain.
5. Write a two-paragraph proposal suggesting your own amendment to the Constitution. Present your proposal to the class, debate any questions, and take a vote for ratification.

PRIMARY SOURCE ANALYSIS

A Living Constitution

Read the text and answer the questions.

Article V of the Constitution allows the Constitution to be amended (changed) if necessary. Since the inclusion of the Bill of Rights, the amendment process has allowed the United States to continually change and improve citizen's rights under the government. For many reasons, the Constitution is often called a "living document."

Excerpts from Amendments

13th Amendment (1865)
"Neither slavery nor involuntary servitude... shall exist with the United States, or any place subject to their jurisdiction."

15th Amendment (1870)
The right of citizens of the United States to vote shall not be denied or abridged by the United States or by any State on account of race, color, or previous condition of servitude.

16th Amendment (1913)
"The Congress shall have power to lay and collect taxes on income, from whatever source derived..."

19th Amendment (1920)
"The right of citizens of the United States to vote shall not be denied or abridged by the United States or by any State on account of sex."

1. What common theme is shared by the 13th and 15th Amendments?
2. Explain the significance of the 13th Amendment. How did it change United States history?
3. What power did the 16th Amendment give to Congress? How does this amendment affect the United States today?
4. Explain the relationship between the 15th and 19th Amendments. What group of people does each amendment affect?
5. In your own words, use the amendments to explain why the Constitution is considered a "living document."

Correlations to Common Core State Standards

For your convenience, correlations are listed page-by-page and for the entire book!

This book is correlated to the <u>Common Core State Standards for English Language Arts</u> grades 3-8, and to Common <u>Core State Standards for Literacy in History, Science, & Technological Subjects</u> grades 6-8.

Correlations are highlighted in gray.

PAGE #	READING	WRITING	LANGUAGE	SPEAKING & LISTENING
	Includes: RI: Reading Informational Text; RH: Reading History	***Includes:*** W: Writing; WHST: Writing History, Science, & Technology	***Includes:*** L: Language; LF: Language Foundational Skills	***Includes:*** SL: Speaking & Listening
2-3	RI RH . **1** **2** 3 **4** 5 6 7 **8** 9 **10**	W WHST . 1 2 3 4 5 6 7 8 9 10	L LF . 1 2 3 **4** 5 **6**	SL . 1 2 3 4 5 6
4	RI RH . **1** **2** 3 4 **5** **6** 7 **8** **9** **10**	W WHST . 1 2 3 4 5 6 7 8 9 10	L LF . 1 2 3 4 5 6	SL . **1** 2 3 **4** 5 **6**
5	RI RH . 1 2 3 **4** **5** 6 7 8 9 **10**	W WHST . **1** 2 3 **4** **5** 6 7 8 **9** **10**	L LF . 1 2 3 4 5 6	SL . 1 2 3 **4** 5 **6**
6-7	RI RH . **1** **2** 3 **4** 5 6 7 8 9 **10**	W WHST 1 2 3 4 5 6 7 8 9 10	L LF 1 2 3 **4** 5 **6**	SL 1 2 3 4 5 6
8	RI RH . **1** **2** 3 4 **5** 6 7 8 9 10	W WHST . 1 2 3 4 5 6 **7** **8** 9 **10**	L LF . 1 2 3 4 5 6	SL . 1 2 3 4 5 6
9	RI RH . **1** **2** 3 4 5 6 7 8 9 **10**	W WHST . 1 2 3 4 5 6 7 8 9 10	L LF . 1 2 3 4 5 6	SL . 1 2 3 4 5 6
10-11	RI RH . **1** **2** 3 **4** 5 6 7 8 9 **10**	W WHST . 1 2 **3** **4** **5** 6 7 8 9 10	L LF . 1 2 3 **4** 5 **6**	SL . 1 2 3 **4** 5 **6**
12-13	RI RH 1 2 3 4 **5** 6 7 8 9 **10**	W WHST 1 2 3 4 5 6 7 8 9 10	L LF 1 2 3 4 5 6	SL 1 2 3 4 5 6
14	RI RH . 1 2 3 **4** 5 6 7 8 9 **10**	W WHST . 1 2 3 4 5 6 7 8 9 10	L LF . 1 2 3 **4** 5 **6**	SL . 1 2 3 4 5 6
15	RI RH . 1 **2** 3 4 5 6 7 8 9 **10**	W WHST . 1 2 3 4 5 6 7 8 9 10	L LF . 1 2 3 4 5 6	SL . 1 2 3 4 5 6
16	RI RH . **1** **2** 3 **4** **5** 6 7 8 **9** **10**	W WHST . 1 2 3 4 5 6 7 8 9 10	L LF . 1 2 3 **4** 5 **6**	SL . **1** 2 3 4 5 **6**
17	RI RH . **1** **2** 3 **4** 5 6 **7** 8 9 **10**	W WHST . 1 **2** 3 **4** 5 6 7 8 **9** **10**	L LF . 1 2 3 **4** 5 **6**	SL . 1 2 3 4 5 6
18	RI RH . 1 2 3 4 **5** 6 7 8 9 **10**	W WHST . 1 2 3 4 5 6 7 8 9 10	L LF . 1 2 3 4 5 6	SL . 1 2 3 4 5 6
19	RI RH . **1** **2** 3 4 5 6 7 8 9 **10**	W WHST . **1** **2** 3 4 5 **6** 7 8 9 **10**	L LF . 1 2 3 4 5 6	SL . 1 2 3 4 5 6
20	RI RH . **1** **2** 3 4 5 6 **7** 8 9 **10**	W WHST . 1 2 3 4 5 6 7 8 9 10	L LF . 1 2 3 4 5 6	SL . 1 2 3 4 5 6
21	RI RH . **1** **2** 3 4 **5** **6** 7 8 **9** **10**	W WHST . **1** 2 3 4 5 6 7 8 9 **10**	L LF . 1 2 3 4 5 6	SL . 1 2 3 4 5 6
22	RI RH . **1** **2** 3 **4** **5** 6 7 8 9 **10**	W WHST . **1** **2** 3 4 5 6 7 8 9 **10**	L LF . 1 2 3 **4** 5 **6**	SL . **1** 2 3 **4** 5 **6**
23	RI RH . **1** **2** 3 4 **5** 6 7 8 9 **10**	W WHST . 1 2 3 4 5 6 7 8 9 10	L LF . 1 2 3 **4** **5** **6**	SL . 1 2 3 4 5 6
	RI RH . 1 2 3 4 5 6 7 8 9 10	W WHST . 1 2 3 4 5 6 7 8 9 10	L LF . 1 2 3 4 5 6	SL . 1 2 3 4 5 6
	RI RH . 1 2 3 4 5 6 7 8 9 10	W WHST . 1 2 3 4 5 6 7 8 9 10	L LF . 1 2 3 4 5 6	SL . 1 2 3 4 5 6
COMPLETE BOOK	RI RH . **1** **2** **3** **4** **5** **6** **7** **8** **9** **10**	W WHST **1** **2** **3** **4** **5** **6** **7** **8** **9** **10**	L LF . 1 2 3 **4** **5** **6**	SL . **1** 2 3 **4** 5 **6**

For the complete Common Core standard identifier, combine your grade + "." + letter code above + "." + number code above.

In addition to the correlations indicated here, the activities may be adapted or expanded to align to additional standards and to meet the diverse needs of your unique students!